Autumn Orange

by Christianne C. Jones

illustrated by Todd Ouren

Special thanks to our advisers for their expertise:

Linda Frichtel, Design Adjunct Faculty
Minneapolis College of Art & Design

Susan Kesselring, M.A., Literacy Educator
Rosemount–Apple Valley–Eagan (Minnesota) School District

PICTURE WINDOW BOOKS
Minneapolis, Minnesota

Editor: Jill Kalz
Designer: Amy Muehlenhardt
Page Production: Brandie Shoemaker
Art Director: Nathan Gassman
The illustrations in this book were created digitally.

Picture Window Books
5115 Excelsior Boulevard
Suite 232
Minneapolis, MN 55416
877-845-8392
www.picturewindowbooks.com

Printed in the United States of America.

Library of Congress Cataloging-in-Publication Data
Jones, Christianne C.
Autumn orange / by Christianne C. Jones ; illustrated by
Todd Ouren.
p. cm. — (Know your colors)
Includes bibliographical references and index.
ISBN-13: 978-1-4048-3108-7 (library binding)
ISBN-10: 1-4048-3108-8 (library binding)
ISBN-13: 978-1-4048-3491-0 (paperback)
ISBN-10: 1-4048-3491-5 (paperback)
1. Orange—Juvenile literature. 2. Color—Juvenile literature.
3. Toy and movable books—Specimens. I. Ouren, Todd, ill.
II. Title.
QC495.5.J655 2006
535.6—dc22   2006027235

The world is filled with COLORS.

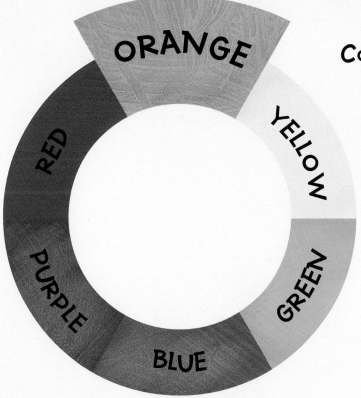

Colors are either primary or secondary. Red, yellow, and blue are primary colors. These are the colors that can't be made by mixing two other colors together. Orange, purple, and green are secondary colors. Secondary colors are made by mixing together two primary colors.

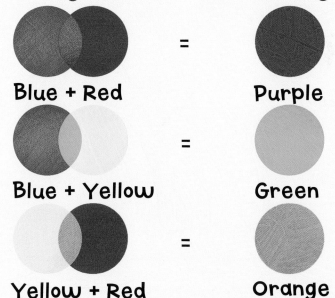

Primary colors		Secondary colors
Blue + Red	=	Purple
Blue + Yellow	=	Green
Yellow + Red	=	Orange

Black and white are neutral colors. They are used to make other colors lighter or darker.

Keep your eyes open for colorful fun!

ORANGE

4

The color ORANGE fills the fields and the trees.
It turns summer to fall as quickly as you please.

FALL FESTI

Many **ORANGE** signs help guide the way.

FESTIVAL

6

7

8

A lazy ORANGE cat rests on the hay.

Plump ORANGE pumpkins brighten the patch.

ORANGE butterflies are hard to catch.

14

A tasty **ORANGE** treat is good to eat.

A black and ORANGE bird
goes TWEET, TWEET, TWEET.

17

Crisp ORANGE leaves begin to sway.

A toasty ORANGE campfire ends the day.

20

The lively fall festival has come to an end.
Does any more ORANGE hide around the bend?

GOODBYE

MAKE A SECONDARY COLOR

WHAT YOU NEED:
- a clear bowl half full of water
- yellow food coloring
- red food coloring
- a spoon

WHAT YOU DO:
1. Add a few drops of yellow food coloring to the water. Then, add a few drops of red.
2. Use the spoon to stir the water to see what color you made!

FUN FACTS

- No word in the English language rhymes with orange.

- Orange is an easy color to see. Joggers and hunters often wear orange vests so they can be easily spotted.

- In many parts of the world, orange stands for heat and energy. People make this connection because fire and the sun both look orange.

- Red, orange, and yellow are called warm colors. Blue, green, and purple are called cool colors.

TO LEARN MORE

AT THE LIBRARY
Gordon, Sharon. *Orange*. New York: Benchmark Books, 2005.

Mitchell, Melanie. *Orange*. Minneapolis: Lerner Publications, 2004.

Schuette, Sarah L. *Orange*. Mankato, Minn.: A+ Books, 2003.

ON THE WEB
FactHound offers a safe, fun way to find Web sites related to this book. All of the sites on FactHound have been researched by our staff.

1. Visit www.facthound.com
2. Type in this special code: 1404831088
3. Click on the FETCH IT button.

Your trusty FactHound will fetch the best sites for you!

Look for all of the books in the Know Your Colors series:

- Autumn Orange
- Big Red Farm
- Camping in Green
- Hello, Yellow!
- Purple Pride
- Splish, Splash, and Blue

24